MW01245644

50 Juice
Recipes for Home

By: Kelly Johnson

Table of Contents

- Cranberry Apple Cooler Juice
- Grapefruit Kiwi Kale Juice
- Beetroot Orange Boost Juice
- Minty Melon Medley Juice
- Cucumber Kiwi Cooler Juice
- Green Grapes Galore Juice
- Lemon Lime Electrolyte Juice
- Orange Basil Bliss Juice
- Strawberry Watermelon Wonder Juice
- Carrot Turmeric Tonic Juice
- Blueberry Spinach Spectacular Juice
- Mango Peach Perfection Juice
- Pineapple Papaya Paradise Juice
- Pear Celery Cleanse Juice
- Green Tea Infused Juice

Green Goddess Juice

Ingredients:

- 2 cups spinach
- 1 cucumber
- 2 stalks celery
- 1 green apple
- 1 lemon, peeled
- 1-inch piece of ginger (optional for added spice)

Instructions:

1. Wash all the vegetables and fruit thoroughly.
2. Cut the cucumber, celery, and apple into chunks that will fit into your juicer chute.
3. Juice the spinach, cucumber, celery, green apple, lemon, and ginger (if using) according to your juicer's instructions.
4. Stir the juice well to combine all the flavors.
5. Serve immediately over ice if desired.

Enjoy your refreshing Green Goddess Juice packed with nutrients!

Citrus Sunrise Juice

Ingredients:

- 2 oranges, peeled
- 1 grapefruit, peeled
- 2 carrots
- 1-inch piece of ginger (optional)

Instructions:

1. Wash and peel the oranges and grapefruit.
2. Wash and chop the carrots into pieces that will fit into your juicer chute.
3. If using ginger, peel it and cut into smaller pieces.
4. Juice the oranges, grapefruit, carrots, and ginger (if using) according to your juicer's instructions.
5. Stir the juice well to combine all the flavors.
6. Serve immediately over ice if desired.

Enjoy the vibrant and refreshing Citrus Sunrise Juice!

Berry Blast Juice

Ingredients:

- 1 cup strawberries
- 1 cup blueberries
- 1 cup raspberries
- 1 cup blackberries
- 1-2 tablespoons honey or agave syrup (optional, for sweetness)
- 1-2 cups cold water or coconut water (adjust for desired consistency)

Instructions:

1. Wash all the berries thoroughly.
2. Hull the strawberries if necessary.
3. Place all the berries into a blender.
4. Add honey or agave syrup (if using) and water or coconut water.
5. Blend on high until smooth and well combined.
6. If desired, strain the juice through a fine mesh sieve to remove seeds (optional).
7. Serve immediately over ice if desired.

Enjoy the refreshing and antioxidant-rich Berry Blast Juice!

Tropical Paradise Juice

Ingredients:

- 1 cup pineapple chunks
- 1 cup mango chunks
- 1 banana, peeled
- 1 orange, peeled
- 1/2 cup coconut water or plain water
- Juice of 1 lime

Instructions:

1. Prepare all the fruits by peeling and cutting them into chunks.
2. Place pineapple chunks, mango chunks, banana, peeled orange segments, coconut water or plain water, and lime juice into a blender.
3. Blend on high speed until smooth and creamy.
4. If the consistency is too thick, add more water or coconut water as needed.
5. Optionally, strain the juice through a fine mesh sieve to achieve a smoother texture.
6. Serve immediately over ice for a refreshing Tropical Paradise Juice experience.

Enjoy the vibrant flavors of the tropics in this delicious juice!

Carrot Ginger Zing Juice

Ingredients:

- 4 medium carrots, washed and ends trimmed
- 1-inch piece of fresh ginger, peeled
- 1 apple (preferably green), cored and cut into wedges
- 1/2 lemon, peeled

Instructions:

1. Wash the carrots thoroughly and trim off the ends.
2. Peel the ginger root.
3. Cut the apple into wedges and remove the core.
4. Peel the lemon.
5. Feed the carrots, ginger, apple wedges, and peeled lemon through a juicer.
6. Stir the juice well to combine all the flavors.
7. Serve immediately over ice if desired.

This Carrot Ginger Zing Juice is refreshing, packed with nutrients, and has a delightful zing from the ginger and lemon. Enjoy!

Apple Kale Cooler Juice

Ingredients:

- 2 green apples, cored and cut into wedges
- 2 cups kale leaves, washed and stems removed
- 1 cucumber, peeled and cut into chunks
- 1 lemon, peeled

Instructions:

1. Wash the apples, kale leaves, cucumber, and lemon thoroughly.
2. Core the apples and cut them into wedges.
3. Peel the cucumber and cut it into chunks.
4. Peel the lemon.
5. Feed the apples, kale leaves, cucumber chunks, and peeled lemon through a juicer.
6. Stir the juice well to combine all the flavors.
7. Serve immediately over ice if desired.

This Apple Kale Cooler Juice is packed with vitamins and minerals from kale and apples, with a refreshing twist from cucumber and lemon. Enjoy this healthy and delicious juice!

Cucumber Mint Refresher Juice

Ingredients:

- 2 cucumbers, peeled if desired and cut into chunks
- 1/2 cup fresh mint leaves
- 1 lime, peeled
- 1-2 tablespoons honey or agave syrup (optional, for sweetness)
- 1-2 cups cold water or coconut water (adjust for desired consistency)

Instructions:

1. Wash the cucumbers, mint leaves, and lime thoroughly.
2. Peel the cucumbers if desired and cut them into chunks.
3. Peel the lime.
4. Place the cucumber chunks, fresh mint leaves, peeled lime, honey or agave syrup (if using), and water or coconut water into a blender.
5. Blend on high speed until smooth and well combined.
6. Optionally, strain the juice through a fine mesh sieve to achieve a smoother texture.
7. Serve immediately over ice if desired.

Enjoy the cooling and refreshing taste of Cucumber Mint Refresher Juice!

Watermelon Basil Bliss Juice

Ingredients:

- 4 cups cubed seedless watermelon
- 1/4 cup fresh basil leaves
- Juice of 1 lime
- 1-2 tablespoons honey or agave syrup (optional, for sweetness)
- Ice cubes (optional)

Instructions:

1. Cut the watermelon into cubes, ensuring there are no seeds.
2. Wash the basil leaves thoroughly.
3. Juice the watermelon cubes and basil leaves together using a juicer.
4. Squeeze in the juice of one lime.
5. Add honey or agave syrup (if using) to sweeten, adjusting to taste.
6. Stir well to combine all flavors.
7. Serve immediately over ice cubes if desired.

This Watermelon Basil Bliss Juice is incredibly refreshing, with a delightful combination of sweet watermelon, herbaceous basil, and a hint of tangy lime. Enjoy this cooling drink on a hot day!

Pineapple Spinach Delight Juice

Ingredients:

- 2 cups fresh spinach leaves
- 2 cups cubed pineapple
- 1 cucumber, peeled and cut into chunks
- 1 lemon, peeled
- 1-inch piece of ginger, peeled (optional for added spice)

Instructions:

1. Wash the spinach leaves, pineapple, cucumber, lemon, and ginger thoroughly.
2. Cut the pineapple into cubes.
3. Peel the cucumber and cut it into chunks.
4. Peel the lemon.
5. If using ginger, peel it and cut into smaller pieces.
6. Feed the spinach leaves, cubed pineapple, cucumber chunks, peeled lemon, and ginger (if using) through a juicer.
7. Stir the juice well to combine all the flavors.
8. Serve immediately over ice if desired.

Enjoy the refreshing and nutritious Pineapple Spinach Delight Juice!

Beetroot Berry Burst Juice

Ingredients:

- 1 medium beetroot, peeled and cut into chunks
- 1 cup strawberries
- 1/2 cup blueberries
- 1/2 cup raspberries
- 1-2 tablespoons honey or agave syrup (optional, for sweetness)
- 1-2 cups cold water or coconut water (adjust for desired consistency)

Instructions:

1. Wash the beetroot, strawberries, blueberries, and raspberries thoroughly.
2. Peel the beetroot and cut it into chunks.
3. Hull the strawberries if necessary.
4. Place the beetroot chunks, strawberries, blueberries, raspberries, honey or agave syrup (if using), and water or coconut water into a blender.
5. Blend on high speed until smooth and well combined.
6. Optionally, strain the juice through a fine mesh sieve to remove seeds (optional).
7. Serve immediately over ice if desired.

Enjoy the vibrant and nutritious Beetroot Berry Burst Juice!

Mango Tango Juice

Ingredients:

- 2 ripe mangoes, peeled and chopped
- 1 orange, peeled and segmented
- 1 banana, peeled
- Juice of 1 lime
- 1-2 cups cold water or coconut water (adjust for desired consistency)
- Ice cubes (optional)

Instructions:

1. Wash and peel the mangoes and orange.
2. Chop the mangoes into chunks.
3. Peel and segment the orange.
4. Peel the banana.
5. Juice the mangoes, orange segments, banana, and lime juice together using a juicer.
6. Add water or coconut water to adjust the consistency and blend again if necessary.
7. Serve immediately over ice cubes if desired.

Enjoy the tropical flavors of this Mango Tango Juice, perfect for a refreshing drink any time of day!

Pomegranate Power Juice

Ingredients:

- 2 cups pomegranate seeds (from 2 large pomegranates)
- 1 apple, cored and cut into chunks
- 1 pear, cored and cut into chunks
- Juice of 1 lemon
- 1-inch piece of ginger, peeled (optional for added spice)
- 1-2 cups cold water or coconut water (adjust for desired consistency)

Instructions:

1. Extract the pomegranate seeds from the pomegranates. You can do this by cutting the fruit in half and gently tapping the back of each half with a spoon over a bowl to release the seeds.
2. Core and cut the apple and pear into chunks.
3. Juice the pomegranate seeds, apple chunks, pear chunks, lemon juice, and ginger (if using) together using a juicer.
4. Add water or coconut water to adjust the consistency and blend again if necessary.
5. Stir well to combine all flavors.
6. Serve immediately over ice cubes if desired.

Enjoy the antioxidant-rich and refreshing Pomegranate Power Juice!

Blueberry Lemonade Juice

Ingredients:

- 2 cups fresh blueberries
- Juice of 2-3 lemons
- 1-2 tablespoons honey or agave syrup (optional, for sweetness)
- 1-2 cups cold water or coconut water (adjust for desired consistency)
- Ice cubes (optional)

Instructions:

1. Wash the blueberries thoroughly.
2. Juice the lemons to extract the lemon juice.
3. Place the blueberries, lemon juice, honey or agave syrup (if using), and water or coconut water into a blender.
4. Blend on high speed until smooth and well combined.
5. Optionally, strain the juice through a fine mesh sieve to remove pulp (optional).
6. Serve immediately over ice cubes if desired.

Enjoy the refreshing and tangy Blueberry Lemonade Juice!

Kiwi Strawberry Surprise Juice

Ingredients:

- 4 kiwis, peeled and chopped
- 1 cup strawberries, hulled and halved
- Juice of 1-2 oranges
- 1-2 tablespoons honey or agave syrup (optional, for sweetness)
- 1-2 cups cold water or coconut water (adjust for desired consistency)
- Ice cubes (optional)

Instructions:

1. Wash and peel the kiwis. Chop them into chunks.
2. Wash the strawberries, remove the hulls, and halve them.
3. Juice the oranges to extract the orange juice.
4. Place the kiwi chunks, halved strawberries, orange juice, honey or agave syrup (if using), and water or coconut water into a blender.
5. Blend on high speed until smooth and well combined.
6. Optionally, strain the juice through a fine mesh sieve to remove seeds or pulp (optional).
7. Serve immediately over ice cubes if desired.

Enjoy the delightful and refreshing Kiwi Strawberry Surprise Juice!

Cranberry Cleanser Juice

Ingredients:

- 2 cups fresh cranberries
- 2 medium apples, cored and cut into chunks
- 1 cucumber, peeled and cut into chunks
- 1 lemon, peeled
- 1-inch piece of ginger, peeled (optional for added spice)
- 1-2 cups cold water or coconut water (adjust for desired consistency)
- Ice cubes (optional)

Instructions:

1. Wash the cranberries, apples, cucumber, lemon, and ginger (if using) thoroughly.
2. Core the apples and cut them into chunks.
3. Peel the cucumber and cut it into chunks.
4. Peel the lemon.
5. If using ginger, peel it and cut into smaller pieces.
6. Juice the cranberries, apple chunks, cucumber chunks, peeled lemon, and ginger (if using) together using a juicer.
7. Add water or coconut water to adjust the consistency and blend again if necessary.
8. Stir well to combine all flavors.
9. Serve immediately over ice cubes if desired.

Enjoy the tart and refreshing Cranberry Cleanser Juice, perfect for a detoxifying drink!

Orange Carrot Energizer Juice

Ingredients:

- 4 large carrots, washed and ends trimmed
- 4 oranges, peeled and segmented
- 1-inch piece of ginger, peeled (optional for added spice)
- 1-2 cups cold water or coconut water (adjust for desired consistency)
- Ice cubes (optional)

Instructions:

1. Wash the carrots thoroughly and trim off the ends.
2. Peel and segment the oranges.
3. If using ginger, peel it and cut into smaller pieces.
4. Juice the carrots, orange segments, and ginger (if using) together using a juicer.
5. Add water or coconut water to adjust the consistency and blend again if necessary.
6. Stir well to combine all flavors.
7. Serve immediately over ice cubes if desired.

Enjoy the zesty and vitamin-packed Orange Carrot Energizer Juice to kick-start your day!

Green Apple Detox Juice

Ingredients:

- 2 green apples, cored and cut into chunks
- 1 cucumber, peeled and cut into chunks
- 2 stalks celery, chopped
- 1 lemon, peeled
- 1-inch piece of ginger, peeled (optional for added spice)
- Handful of fresh parsley or cilantro (optional)
- 1-2 cups cold water or coconut water (adjust for desired consistency)
- Ice cubes (optional)

Instructions:

1. Wash all the produce thoroughly.
2. Core the green apples and cut them into chunks.
3. Peel the cucumber and cut it into chunks.
4. Chop the celery stalks.
5. Peel the lemon.
6. If using ginger, peel it and cut into smaller pieces.
7. Optional: Add a handful of fresh parsley or cilantro for additional detox benefits.
8. Juice the green apples, cucumber chunks, celery, peeled lemon, ginger (if using), and herbs (if using) together using a juicer.
9. Add water or coconut water to adjust the consistency and blend again if necessary.
10. Stir well to combine all flavors.
11. Serve immediately over ice cubes if desired.

Enjoy the refreshing and detoxifying Green Apple Detox Juice!

Turmeric Tonic Juice

Ingredients:

- 1-2 inches of fresh turmeric root, peeled
- 1-2 inches of fresh ginger root, peeled
- 2-3 medium carrots, washed and ends trimmed
- 1 orange, peeled and segmented
- Juice of 1 lemon
- Pinch of black pepper (optional, to enhance turmeric absorption)
- 1-2 cups cold water or coconut water (adjust for desired consistency)
- Ice cubes (optional)

Instructions:

1. Wash and peel the turmeric and ginger roots.
2. Wash and trim the carrots.
3. Peel and segment the orange.
4. Juice the turmeric, ginger, carrots, orange segments, and lemon juice together using a juicer.
5. Optional: Add a pinch of black pepper to the juice to enhance the absorption of turmeric's beneficial compounds.
6. Add water or coconut water to adjust the consistency and blend again if necessary.
7. Stir well to combine all flavors.
8. Serve immediately over ice cubes if desired.

Enjoy the spicy and invigorating Turmeric Tonic Juice, known for its anti-inflammatory properties and vibrant flavor!

Cantaloupe Cucumber Cooler Juice

Ingredients:

- 1/2 medium cantaloupe, seeds removed and flesh scooped into chunks
- 1 cucumber, peeled and cut into chunks
- Juice of 1 lime
- Handful of fresh mint leaves
- 1-2 tablespoons honey or agave syrup (optional, for sweetness)
- 1-2 cups cold water or coconut water (adjust for desired consistency)
- Ice cubes (optional)

Instructions:

1. Scoop out the flesh of the cantaloupe and cut it into chunks.
2. Peel the cucumber and cut it into chunks.
3. Juice the cantaloupe chunks and cucumber chunks together using a juicer.
4. Add the juice of one lime to the juicer.
5. Optional: Add a handful of fresh mint leaves for a refreshing twist.
6. Add honey or agave syrup (if using) to sweeten, adjusting to taste.
7. Blend on high speed until smooth and well combined.
8. Add water or coconut water to adjust the consistency and blend again if necessary.
9. Stir well to combine all flavors.
10. Serve immediately over ice cubes if desired.

Enjoy the cool and hydrating Cantaloupe Cucumber Cooler Juice!

Grapefruit Mint Reviver Juice

Ingredients:

- 2 grapefruits, peeled and segmented
- Handful of fresh mint leaves
- 1 cucumber, peeled and cut into chunks
- 1 inch piece of ginger, peeled (optional)
- 1-2 tablespoons honey or agave syrup (optional, for sweetness)
- 1-2 cups cold water or coconut water (adjust for desired consistency)
- Ice cubes (optional)

Instructions:

1. Peel and segment the grapefruits.
2. Wash the fresh mint leaves.
3. Peel the cucumber and cut it into chunks.
4. If using ginger, peel it and cut into smaller pieces.
5. Juice the grapefruit segments, fresh mint leaves, cucumber chunks, and ginger (if using) together using a juicer.
6. Add honey or agave syrup (if using) to sweeten, adjusting to taste.
7. Blend on high speed until smooth and well combined.
8. Add water or coconut water to adjust the consistency and blend again if necessary.
9. Stir well to combine all flavors.
10. Serve immediately over ice cubes if desired.

Enjoy the refreshing and revitalizing Grapefruit Mint Reviver Juice!

Celery Cilantro Cleansing Juice

Ingredients:

- 4-5 stalks of celery
- Handful of fresh cilantro leaves
- 1 cucumber, peeled and cut into chunks
- 1 green apple, cored and cut into chunks
- Juice of 1 lemon
- 1-inch piece of ginger, peeled (optional for added spice)
- 1-2 cups cold water or coconut water (adjust for desired consistency)
- Ice cubes (optional)

Instructions:

1. Wash all the produce thoroughly.
2. Cut the celery stalks into smaller pieces.
3. Wash the cilantro leaves.
4. Peel the cucumber and cut it into chunks.
5. Core and cut the green apple into chunks.
6. Juice the celery pieces, cilantro leaves, cucumber chunks, green apple chunks, lemon juice, and ginger (if using) together using a juicer.
7. Add water or coconut water to adjust the consistency and blend again if necessary.
8. Stir well to combine all flavors.
9. Serve immediately over ice cubes if desired.

Enjoy the cleansing and refreshing Celery Cilantro Cleansing Juice!

Lemon Ginger Immunity Booster Juice

Ingredients:

- 2 lemons, peeled and segmented
- 1-inch piece of ginger, peeled
- 2-3 carrots, washed and ends trimmed
- 1 orange, peeled and segmented
- 1-2 tablespoons honey or agave syrup (optional, for sweetness)
- 1-2 cups cold water or coconut water (adjust for desired consistency)
- Ice cubes (optional)

Instructions:

1. Peel and segment the lemons and oranges.
2. Peel the ginger and cut it into smaller pieces.
3. Wash and trim the carrots.
4. Juice the lemon segments, ginger pieces, carrots, and orange segments together using a juicer.
5. Add honey or agave syrup (if using) to sweeten, adjusting to taste.
6. Blend on high speed until smooth and well combined.
7. Add water or coconut water to adjust the consistency and blend again if necessary.
8. Stir well to combine all flavors.
9. Serve immediately over ice cubes if desired.

Enjoy the zesty and immune-boosting Lemon Ginger Immunity Booster Juice!

Spinach Pear Perfection Juice

Ingredients:

- 2 cups fresh spinach leaves
- 2 ripe pears, cored and cut into chunks
- 1 cucumber, peeled and cut into chunks
- 1 lemon, peeled
- 1-inch piece of ginger, peeled (optional for added spice)
- 1-2 cups cold water or coconut water (adjust for desired consistency)
- Ice cubes (optional)

Instructions:

1. Wash all the produce thoroughly.
2. Remove the cores from the pears and cut them into chunks.
3. Peel the cucumber and cut it into chunks.
4. Peel the lemon.
5. If using ginger, peel it and cut into smaller pieces.
6. Juice the spinach leaves, pear chunks, cucumber chunks, peeled lemon, and ginger (if using) together using a juicer.
7. Add water or coconut water to adjust the consistency and blend again if necessary.
8. Stir well to combine all flavors.
9. Serve immediately over ice cubes if desired.

Enjoy the refreshing and nutrient-packed Spinach Pear Perfection Juice!

Papaya Passion Juice

Ingredients:

- 1 small ripe papaya, peeled, seeded, and cubed
- 1 cup pineapple chunks
- 1 orange, peeled and segmented
- Juice of 1 lime
- 1-2 tablespoons honey or agave syrup (optional, for sweetness)
- 1-2 cups cold water or coconut water (adjust for desired consistency)
- Ice cubes (optional)

Instructions:

1. Peel, seed, and cube the papaya.
2. Cut the pineapple into chunks.
3. Peel and segment the orange.
4. Juice the papaya cubes, pineapple chunks, orange segments, and lime juice together using a juicer.
5. Add honey or agave syrup (if using) to sweeten, adjusting to taste.
6. Blend on high speed until smooth and well combined.
7. Add water or coconut water to adjust the consistency and blend again if necessary.
8. Stir well to combine all flavors.
9. Serve immediately over ice cubes if desired.

Enjoy the tropical and refreshing Papaya Passion Juice!

Tomato Basil Brunch Juice

Ingredients:

- 4-5 ripe tomatoes
- Handful of fresh basil leaves
- 1 cucumber, peeled and cut into chunks
- 1 celery stalk, chopped
- Juice of 1 lemon
- 1-2 tablespoons honey or agave syrup (optional, for sweetness)
- Dash of hot sauce (optional, for spice)
- 1-2 cups cold water or coconut water (adjust for desired consistency)
- Ice cubes (optional)

Instructions:

1. Wash all the produce thoroughly.
2. Core the tomatoes and cut them into chunks.
3. Wash the fresh basil leaves.
4. Peel the cucumber and cut it into chunks.
5. Chop the celery stalk.
6. Juice the tomato chunks, fresh basil leaves, cucumber chunks, celery, lemon juice, and hot sauce (if using) together using a juicer.
7. Add honey or agave syrup (if using) to sweeten, adjusting to taste.
8. Blend on high speed until smooth and well combined.
9. Add water or coconut water to adjust the consistency and blend again if necessary.
10. Stir well to combine all flavors.
11. Serve immediately over ice cubes if desired.

Enjoy the savory and brunch-worthy Tomato Basil Brunch Juice!

Bell Pepper Beet Blast Juice

Ingredients:

- 1 large beetroot, peeled and chopped
- 1 red bell pepper, seeded and chopped
- 1 yellow bell pepper, seeded and chopped
- 1 orange, peeled and segmented
- Juice of 1 lemon
- 1-inch piece of ginger, peeled (optional for added spice)
- 1-2 cups cold water or coconut water (adjust for desired consistency)
- Ice cubes (optional)

Instructions:

1. Wash all the produce thoroughly.
2. Peel and chop the beetroot.
3. Seed and chop the red and yellow bell peppers.
4. Peel and segment the orange.
5. Juice the beetroot, red bell pepper, yellow bell pepper, orange segments, lemon juice, and ginger (if using) together using a juicer.
6. Add water or coconut water to adjust the consistency and blend again if necessary.
7. Stir well to combine all flavors.
8. Serve immediately over ice cubes if desired.

Enjoy the vibrant and nutritious Bell Pepper Beet Blast Juice!

Kale Pineapple Punch Juice

Ingredients:

- 2 cups fresh kale leaves, washed and stems removed
- 2 cups pineapple chunks
- 1 cucumber, peeled and cut into chunks
- 1 green apple, cored and cut into chunks
- Juice of 1 lemon
- 1-inch piece of ginger, peeled (optional for added spice)
- 1-2 cups cold water or coconut water (adjust for desired consistency)
- Ice cubes (optional)

Instructions:

1. Wash the kale leaves thoroughly and remove any tough stems.
2. Cut the pineapple into chunks.
3. Peel the cucumber and cut it into chunks.
4. Core and cut the green apple into chunks.
5. Juice the kale leaves, pineapple chunks, cucumber chunks, green apple chunks, lemon juice, and ginger (if using) together using a juicer.
6. Add water or coconut water to adjust the consistency and blend again if necessary.
7. Stir well to combine all flavors.
8. Serve immediately over ice cubes if desired.

Enjoy the refreshing and nutritious Kale Pineapple Punch Juice!

Watermelon Mint Mojito Juice

Ingredients:

- 4 cups cubed seedless watermelon
- Juice of 2-3 limes
- Handful of fresh mint leaves
- 1-2 tablespoons honey or agave syrup (optional, for sweetness)
- 1-2 cups cold water or coconut water (adjust for desired consistency)
- Ice cubes (optional)

Instructions:

1. Cut the watermelon into cubes, ensuring there are no seeds.
2. Juice the limes to extract the lime juice.
3. Wash the fresh mint leaves.
4. Place the cubed watermelon, lime juice, fresh mint leaves, and honey or agave syrup (if using) into a blender.
5. Blend on high speed until smooth and well combined.
6. Add water or coconut water to adjust the consistency and blend again if necessary.
7. Stir well to combine all flavors.
8. Serve immediately over ice cubes if desired.

Enjoy the refreshing and minty Watermelon Mint Mojito Juice, perfect for a summer day!

Carrot Orange Sunshine Juice

Ingredients:

- 4-5 large carrots, washed and ends trimmed
- 4 oranges, peeled and segmented
- Juice of 1 lemon
- 1-inch piece of ginger, peeled (optional for added spice)
- 1-2 tablespoons honey or agave syrup (optional, for sweetness)
- 1-2 cups cold water or coconut water (adjust for desired consistency)
- Ice cubes (optional)

Instructions:

1. Wash the carrots thoroughly and trim off the ends.
2. Peel and segment the oranges.
3. Juice the carrots, orange segments, and lemon juice together using a juicer.
4. If using ginger, peel it and cut into smaller pieces, then add to the juicer.
5. Add honey or agave syrup (if using) to sweeten, adjusting to taste.
6. Blend on high speed until smooth and well combined.
7. Add water or coconut water to adjust the consistency and blend again if necessary.
8. Stir well to combine all flavors.
9. Serve immediately over ice cubes if desired.

Enjoy the bright and sunny Carrot Orange Sunshine Juice!

Blueberry Lavender Lemonade Juice

Ingredients:

- 2 cups fresh blueberries
- Juice of 3-4 lemons
- 1 tablespoon dried culinary lavender (or 2-3 fresh lavender sprigs)
- 1-2 tablespoons honey or agave syrup (adjust for sweetness)
- 1-2 cups cold water or sparkling water
- Ice cubes

Instructions:

1. Rinse the blueberries thoroughly.
2. Juice the lemons to extract the lemon juice.
3. In a small pot, combine the lavender with 1 cup of water. Bring to a boil, then reduce heat and let it simmer for 5 minutes. Remove from heat and let it cool down. Strain the lavender-infused water to remove the lavender flowers, and set aside.
4. In a blender, combine the blueberries, lemon juice, lavender-infused water, and honey or agave syrup.
5. Blend until smooth.
6. Pour the mixture through a fine mesh sieve to remove any solids.
7. Transfer the strained juice into a pitcher.
8. Add 1-2 cups of cold water or sparkling water to dilute, depending on your desired taste.
9. Stir well to combine.
10. Serve over ice cubes.

This Blueberry Lavender Lemonade Juice offers a unique blend of sweet blueberries, tart lemon, and aromatic lavender, making it a refreshing and sophisticated drink. Adjust sweetness and dilution according to your preference. Enjoy!

Mango Mint Madness Juice

Ingredients:

- 2 ripe mangoes, peeled and chopped
- Handful of fresh mint leaves
- Juice of 1-2 limes
- 1-2 tablespoons honey or agave syrup (optional, for sweetness)
- 1-2 cups cold water or coconut water (adjust for desired consistency)
- Ice cubes (optional)

Instructions:

1. Peel and chop the ripe mangoes.
2. Wash the fresh mint leaves.
3. Juice the limes to extract the lime juice.
4. In a blender, combine the chopped mangoes, fresh mint leaves, lime juice, and honey or agave syrup (if using).
5. Blend until smooth.
6. Add cold water or coconut water to adjust the consistency and blend again if necessary.
7. Stir well to combine all flavors.
8. Serve immediately over ice cubes if desired.

This Mango Mint Madness Juice is refreshing and packed with tropical flavors from mangoes and the coolness of mint. Adjust sweetness and consistency to suit your taste preferences. Enjoy!

Raspberry Lime Refresher Juice

Ingredients:

- 2 cups fresh raspberries
- Juice of 2-3 limes
- 1-2 tablespoons honey or agave syrup (optional, for sweetness)
- 1-2 cups cold water or coconut water (adjust for desired consistency)
- Ice cubes (optional)

Instructions:

1. Rinse the fresh raspberries thoroughly.
2. Juice the limes to extract the lime juice.
3. In a blender, combine the fresh raspberries and lime juice.
4. Add honey or agave syrup (if using) to sweeten, adjusting to taste.
5. Blend until smooth.
6. Add cold water or coconut water to adjust the consistency and blend again if necessary.
7. Stir well to combine all flavors.
8. Serve immediately over ice cubes if desired.

This Raspberry Lime Refresher Juice is tangy, refreshing, and packed with antioxidants from raspberries and the zesty kick of lime. Adjust sweetness and consistency to suit your taste preferences. Enjoy!

Apple Cinnamon Spice Juice

Ingredients:

- 4 apples, cored and cut into chunks (choose sweet varieties like Gala or Fuji)
- 1 teaspoon ground cinnamon
- 1/2 teaspoon ground nutmeg
- 1/2 teaspoon ground ginger
- Juice of 1 lemon
- 1-2 tablespoons honey or agave syrup (optional, for sweetness)
- 1-2 cups cold water or coconut water (adjust for desired consistency)
- Ice cubes (optional)

Instructions:

1. Core and cut the apples into chunks.
2. In a blender, combine the apple chunks, ground cinnamon, nutmeg, ginger, lemon juice, and honey or agave syrup (if using).
3. Blend until smooth.
4. Add cold water or coconut water to adjust the consistency and blend again if necessary.
5. Stir well to combine all flavors.
6. Serve immediately over ice cubes if desired.

This Apple Cinnamon Spice Juice is warm and comforting, perfect for cooler weather or as a festive treat. Adjust the sweetness and spice levels to suit your taste preferences. Enjoy!

Pineapple Ginger Zinger Juice

Ingredients:

- 2 cups pineapple chunks
- 1-inch piece of ginger, peeled
- Juice of 1-2 limes
- 1-2 tablespoons honey or agave syrup (optional, for sweetness)
- 1-2 cups cold water or coconut water (adjust for desired consistency)
- Ice cubes (optional)

Instructions:

1. Peel and cut the pineapple into chunks.
2. Peel the ginger and cut it into smaller pieces.
3. Juice the pineapple chunks and ginger together using a juicer.
4. Juice the limes to extract the lime juice.
5. In a blender, combine the pineapple and ginger juice with lime juice and honey or agave syrup (if using).
6. Blend until smooth.
7. Add cold water or coconut water to adjust the consistency and blend again if necessary.
8. Stir well to combine all flavors.
9. Serve immediately over ice cubes if desired.

Enjoy the zesty and refreshing Pineapple Ginger Zinger Juice! Adjust sweetness and consistency to suit your taste preferences.

Pear Spinach Soother Juice

Ingredients:

- 2 ripe pears, cored and cut into chunks
- 2 cups fresh spinach leaves, washed
- Juice of 1-2 lemons
- 1-inch piece of ginger, peeled (optional for added spice)
- 1-2 tablespoons honey or agave syrup (optional, for sweetness)
- 1-2 cups cold water or coconut water (adjust for desired consistency)
- Ice cubes (optional)

Instructions:

1. Wash the pears thoroughly, remove the cores, and cut them into chunks.
2. Wash the fresh spinach leaves.
3. Juice the lemons to extract the lemon juice.
4. Peel the ginger (if using) and cut it into smaller pieces.
5. In a juicer, juice the pear chunks, spinach leaves, lemon juice, and ginger (if using).
6. Add honey or agave syrup (if using) to sweeten, adjusting to taste.
7. Blend on high speed until smooth and well combined.
8. Add cold water or coconut water to adjust the consistency and blend again if necessary.
9. Stir well to combine all flavors.
10. Serve immediately over ice cubes if desired.

Enjoy the soothing and nutritious Pear Spinach Soother Juice! Adjust sweetness and consistency according to your preference.

Cranberry Apple Cooler Juice

Ingredients:

- 2 cups cranberries, fresh or frozen
- 2 apples, cored and cut into chunks
- 1 cucumber, peeled and cut into chunks
- Juice of 1-2 lemons
- 1-2 tablespoons honey or agave syrup (optional, for sweetness)
- 1-2 cups cold water or coconut water (adjust for desired consistency)
- Ice cubes (optional)

Instructions:

1. Wash the cranberries thoroughly.
2. Core the apples and cut them into chunks.
3. Peel the cucumber and cut it into chunks.
4. Juice the cranberries, apple chunks, and cucumber chunks together using a juicer.
5. Juice the lemons to extract the lemon juice.
6. In a blender, combine the cranberry, apple, and cucumber juice with lemon juice and honey or agave syrup (if using).
7. Blend until smooth.
8. Add cold water or coconut water to adjust the consistency and blend again if necessary.
9. Stir well to combine all flavors.
10. Serve immediately over ice cubes if desired.

Enjoy the crisp and cooling Cranberry Apple Cooler Juice! Adjust sweetness and consistency according to your taste preferences.

Grapefruit Kiwi Kale Juice

Ingredients:

- 2 grapefruits, peeled and segmented
- 2 kiwis, peeled and sliced
- 2 cups kale leaves, washed and stems removed
- 1-2 tablespoons honey or agave syrup (optional, for sweetness)
- 1-2 cups cold water or coconut water (adjust for desired consistency)
- Ice cubes (optional)

Instructions:

1. Peel and segment the grapefruits.
2. Peel and slice the kiwis.
3. Wash the kale leaves thoroughly and remove the stems.
4. Juice the grapefruit segments, kiwi slices, and kale leaves together using a juicer.
5. In a blender, combine the grapefruit, kiwi, and kale juice.
6. Add honey or agave syrup (if using) to sweeten, adjusting to taste.
7. Blend until smooth.
8. Add cold water or coconut water to adjust the consistency and blend again if necessary.
9. Stir well to combine all flavors.
10. Serve immediately over ice cubes if desired.

Enjoy the tangy and nutritious Grapefruit Kiwi Kale Juice! Adjust sweetness and consistency according to your preference.

Beetroot Orange Boost Juice

Ingredients:

- 1 large beetroot, peeled and chopped
- 3 oranges, peeled and segmented
- Juice of 1 lemon
- 1-inch piece of ginger, peeled (optional for added spice)
- 1-2 tablespoons honey or agave syrup (optional, for sweetness)
- 1-2 cups cold water or coconut water (adjust for desired consistency)
- Ice cubes (optional)

Instructions:

1. Wash and peel the beetroot, then chop it into chunks.
2. Peel and segment the oranges.
3. Juice the beetroot chunks and orange segments together using a juicer.
4. Juice the lemon to extract the lemon juice.
5. If using ginger, peel it and cut it into smaller pieces, then add to the juicer.
6. In a blender, combine the beetroot and orange juice with lemon juice and honey or agave syrup (if using).
7. Blend until smooth.
8. Add cold water or coconut water to adjust the consistency and blend again if necessary.
9. Stir well to combine all flavors.
10. Serve immediately over ice cubes if desired.

This Beetroot Orange Boost Juice is vibrant and packed with vitamins and antioxidants. Adjust sweetness and consistency to your liking and enjoy this refreshing boost!

Minty Melon Medley Juice

Ingredients:

- 4 cups cubed honeydew melon
- 2 cups cubed cantaloupe melon
- Handful of fresh mint leaves
- Juice of 1-2 limes
- 1-2 tablespoons honey or agave syrup (optional, for sweetness)
- 1-2 cups cold water or coconut water (adjust for desired consistency)
- Ice cubes (optional)

Instructions:

1. Cube the honeydew and cantaloupe melons, ensuring they are seedless.
2. Wash the fresh mint leaves.
3. Juice the limes to extract the lime juice.
4. In a blender, combine the cubed honeydew melon, cubed cantaloupe melon, fresh mint leaves, lime juice, and honey or agave syrup (if using).
5. Blend until smooth.
6. Add cold water or coconut water to adjust the consistency and blend again if necessary.
7. Stir well to combine all flavors.
8. Serve immediately over ice cubes if desired.

Enjoy the refreshing and minty Minty Melon Medley Juice! Adjust sweetness and consistency according to your preference.

Cucumber Kiwi Cooler Juice

Ingredients:

- 2 cucumbers, peeled and chopped
- 4 kiwis, peeled and chopped
- Juice of 1-2 limes
- Handful of fresh mint leaves
- 1-2 tablespoons honey or agave syrup (optional, for sweetness)
- 1-2 cups cold water or coconut water (adjust for desired consistency)
- Ice cubes (optional)

Instructions:

1. Peel and chop the cucumbers.
2. Peel and chop the kiwis.
3. Juice the limes to extract the lime juice.
4. Wash the fresh mint leaves.
5. In a blender, combine the chopped cucumbers, chopped kiwis, lime juice, fresh mint leaves, and honey or agave syrup (if using).
6. Blend until smooth.
7. Add cold water or coconut water to adjust the consistency and blend again if necessary.
8. Stir well to combine all flavors.
9. Serve immediately over ice cubes if desired.

Enjoy the cool and refreshing Cucumber Kiwi Cooler Juice! Adjust sweetness and consistency to suit your taste preferences.

Green Grapes Galore Juice

Ingredients:

- 2 cups green grapes
- 2 green apples, cored and cut into chunks
- 1 cucumber, peeled and cut into chunks
- Handful of spinach leaves
- Juice of 1-2 limes
- 1-2 tablespoons honey or agave syrup (optional, for sweetness)
- 1-2 cups cold water or coconut water (adjust for desired consistency)
- Ice cubes (optional)

Instructions:

1. Wash the green grapes thoroughly.
2. Core and cut the green apples into chunks.
3. Peel and cut the cucumber into chunks.
4. Wash the spinach leaves.
5. Juice the green grapes, green apples, cucumber chunks, and spinach leaves together using a juicer.
6. Juice the limes to extract the lime juice.
7. In a blender, combine the grape, apple, cucumber, and spinach juice with lime juice and honey or agave syrup (if using).
8. Blend until smooth.
9. Add cold water or coconut water to adjust the consistency and blend again if necessary.
10. Stir well to combine all flavors.
11. Serve immediately over ice cubes if desired.

Enjoy the refreshing and nutritious Green Grapes Galore Juice! Adjust sweetness and consistency according to your preference.

Lemon Lime Electrolyte Juice

Ingredients:

- Juice of 2 lemons
- Juice of 2 limes
- 2 cups coconut water (natural electrolyte source)
- 1-2 tablespoons honey or agave syrup (optional, for sweetness)
- Pinch of sea salt (to enhance electrolytes)
- Ice cubes (optional)

Instructions:

1. Juice the lemons and limes to extract the citrus juice.
2. In a pitcher or blender, combine the lemon juice, lime juice, coconut water, honey or agave syrup (if using), and a pinch of sea salt.
3. Stir or blend well to ensure all ingredients are mixed thoroughly.
4. Taste and adjust sweetness or saltiness if necessary.
5. Serve chilled over ice cubes if desired.

This Lemon Lime Electrolyte Juice is perfect for rehydrating after exercise or on a hot day, providing natural electrolytes and a refreshing citrus flavor. Adjust sweetness and saltiness according to your taste preference.

Orange Basil Bliss Juice

Ingredients:

- 4 oranges, peeled and segmented
- Handful of fresh basil leaves
- Juice of 1-2 lemons
- 1-2 tablespoons honey or agave syrup (optional, for sweetness)
- 1-2 cups cold water or coconut water (adjust for desired consistency)
- Ice cubes (optional)

Instructions:

1. Peel and segment the oranges.
2. Wash the fresh basil leaves.
3. Juice the lemons to extract the lemon juice.
4. In a blender, combine the orange segments, fresh basil leaves, lemon juice, and honey or agave syrup (if using).
5. Blend until smooth.
6. Add cold water or coconut water to adjust the consistency and blend again if necessary.
7. Stir well to combine all flavors.
8. Serve immediately over ice cubes if desired.

Enjoy the refreshing and aromatic Orange Basil Bliss Juice! Adjust sweetness and consistency according to your taste preferences.

Strawberry Watermelon Wonder Juice

Ingredients:

- 2 cups fresh strawberries, hulled
- 4 cups cubed seedless watermelon
- Juice of 1-2 limes
- 1-2 tablespoons honey or agave syrup (optional, for sweetness)
- 1-2 cups cold water or coconut water (adjust for desired consistency)
- Ice cubes (optional)

Instructions:

1. Wash the strawberries and remove the hulls.
2. Cut the watermelon into cubes, ensuring it's seedless.
3. Juice the limes to extract the lime juice.
4. In a blender, combine the strawberries, watermelon cubes, lime juice, and honey or agave syrup (if using).
5. Blend until smooth.
6. Add cold water or coconut water to adjust the consistency and blend again if necessary.
7. Stir well to combine all flavors.
8. Serve immediately over ice cubes if desired.

Enjoy the delightful and refreshing Strawberry Watermelon Wonder Juice! Adjust sweetness and consistency according to your preference.

Carrot Turmeric Tonic Juice

Ingredients:

- 4-5 carrots, washed and trimmed
- 1-inch piece of fresh turmeric root, peeled (or 1 teaspoon ground turmeric)
- Juice of 1-2 oranges
- Juice of 1 lemon
- 1-2 tablespoons honey or agave syrup (optional, for sweetness)
- Pinch of black pepper (to enhance turmeric absorption)
- 1-2 cups cold water or coconut water (adjust for desired consistency)
- Ice cubes (optional)

Instructions:

1. Wash and trim the carrots, and peel the turmeric root.
2. Juice the carrots and turmeric root together using a juicer.
3. Juice the oranges and lemon to extract the citrus juice.
4. In a blender, combine the carrot and turmeric juice with the orange juice, lemon juice, honey or agave syrup (if using), and a pinch of black pepper.
5. Blend until smooth.
6. Add cold water or coconut water to adjust the consistency and blend again if necessary.
7. Stir well to combine all flavors.
8. Serve immediately over ice cubes if desired.

This Carrot Turmeric Tonic Juice is not only delicious but also packed with antioxidants and anti-inflammatory properties from the carrots and turmeric. Adjust sweetness and consistency to suit your taste preferences. Enjoy the vibrant and healthful benefits of this tonic!

Blueberry Spinach Spectacular Juice

Ingredients:

- 2 cups fresh blueberries
- 2 cups fresh spinach leaves, washed
- 1 cucumber, peeled and cut into chunks
- Juice of 1-2 lemons
- 1-2 tablespoons honey or agave syrup (optional, for sweetness)
- 1-2 cups cold water or coconut water (adjust for desired consistency)
- Ice cubes (optional)

Instructions:

1. Rinse the fresh blueberries and spinach leaves thoroughly.
2. Peel and cut the cucumber into chunks.
3. Juice the blueberries, spinach leaves, and cucumber chunks together using a juicer.
4. Juice the lemons to extract the lemon juice.
5. In a blender, combine the blueberry, spinach, and cucumber juice with lemon juice and honey or agave syrup (if using).
6. Blend until smooth.
7. Add cold water or coconut water to adjust the consistency and blend again if necessary.
8. Stir well to combine all flavors.
9. Serve immediately over ice cubes if desired.

This Blueberry Spinach Spectacular Juice is refreshing and nutritious, packed with antioxidants and vitamins from the blueberries and spinach. Adjust sweetness and consistency according to your taste preferences. Enjoy!

Mango Peach Perfection Juice

Ingredients:

- 2 ripe mangoes, peeled and chopped
- 2 ripe peaches, pitted and chopped
- Juice of 1-2 oranges
- Juice of 1-2 limes
- 1-2 tablespoons honey or agave syrup (optional, for sweetness)
- 1-2 cups cold water or coconut water (adjust for desired consistency)
- Ice cubes (optional)

Instructions:

1. Peel and chop the ripe mangoes.
2. Pit and chop the ripe peaches.
3. Juice the oranges and limes to extract the citrus juice.
4. In a blender, combine the chopped mangoes, chopped peaches, orange juice, lime juice, and honey or agave syrup (if using).
5. Blend until smooth.
6. Add cold water or coconut water to adjust the consistency and blend again if necessary.
7. Stir well to combine all flavors.
8. Serve immediately over ice cubes if desired.

This Mango Peach Perfection Juice is refreshing and bursting with tropical flavors from mangoes and the sweet tanginess of peaches. Adjust sweetness and consistency to suit your taste preferences. Enjoy this delicious and nutritious juice!

Pineapple Papaya Paradise Juice

Ingredients:

- 2 cups pineapple chunks
- 2 cups papaya chunks
- Juice of 1-2 oranges
- Juice of 1-2 limes
- 1-2 tablespoons honey or agave syrup (optional, for sweetness)
- 1-2 cups cold water or coconut water (adjust for desired consistency)
- Ice cubes (optional)

Instructions:

1. Peel and cut the pineapple into chunks.
2. Peel and cut the papaya into chunks, removing seeds.
3. Juice the oranges and limes to extract the citrus juice.
4. In a blender, combine the pineapple chunks, papaya chunks, orange juice, lime juice, and honey or agave syrup (if using).
5. Blend until smooth.
6. Add cold water or coconut water to adjust the consistency and blend again if needed.
7. Stir well to combine all flavors.
8. Serve immediately over ice cubes if desired.

This Pineapple Papaya Paradise Juice is tropical, refreshing, and packed with vitamins. Adjust sweetness and consistency according to your taste preferences. Enjoy the taste of paradise in a glass!

Pear Celery Cleanse Juice

Ingredients:

- 2 pears, cored and chopped
- 4 stalks of celery, chopped
- Juice of 1-2 lemons
- 1-inch piece of ginger, peeled (optional)
- 1-2 tablespoons honey or agave syrup (optional, for sweetness)
- 1-2 cups cold water or coconut water (adjust for desired consistency)
- Ice cubes (optional)

Instructions:

1. Core and chop the pears.
2. Chop the celery stalks.
3. Juice the lemons to extract the lemon juice.
4. If using ginger, peel it and cut it into smaller pieces.
5. In a juicer, juice the pears, celery, lemon juice, and ginger (if using).
6. In a blender, combine the juice with honey or agave syrup (if using).
7. Add cold water or coconut water to adjust the consistency.
8. Stir well to combine all flavors.
9. Serve immediately over ice cubes if desired.

This Pear Celery Cleanse Juice is refreshing and nutritious, perfect for a cleansing boost. Adjust sweetness and consistency according to your taste preferences. Enjoy!

Green Tea Infused Juice

Ingredients:

- 2 cups brewed green tea, cooled to room temperature
- 1 cup pineapple chunks
- 1 cup cucumber slices
- Juice of 1-2 lemons
- 1-2 tablespoons honey or agave syrup (optional, for sweetness)
- Ice cubes (optional)

Instructions:

1. Brew green tea and allow it to cool to room temperature.
2. In a blender, combine the cooled green tea, pineapple chunks, cucumber slices, and lemon juice.
3. Add honey or agave syrup (if using) for sweetness.
4. Blend until smooth.
5. If the mixture is too thick, add cold water or coconut water to adjust the consistency and blend again if necessary.
6. Stir well to combine all flavors.
7. Serve immediately over ice cubes if desired.

Enjoy the refreshing and antioxidant-rich Green Tea Infused Juice! Adjust sweetness and consistency according to your preference. This juice provides a refreshing twist with the added health benefits of green tea.

Printed in the USA
CPSIA information can be obtained
at www.ICGtesting.com
CBHW081801180724
11673CB00021B/508